WILDERNESS
OF
MIRRORS

Charles Evered

BROADWAY PLAY PUBLISHING INC
56 E 81st St., NY NY 10028-0202
212 772-8334 fax: 212 772-8358
http://www.BroadwayPlayPubl.com

WILDERNESS OF MIRRORS
© Copyright 2004 by Charles Evered

First printing: April 2004
Second printing: February 2005

I S B N: 0-88145-233-5

Book design: Marie Donovan
Word processing: Microsoft Word for Windows
Typographic controls: Xerox Ventura Publisher 2.0 P E
Typeface: Palatino
Printed and bound in the U S A

ABOUT THE AUTHOR

Charles Evered is an author and journalist who has written for *The London Times* and *The Star Ledger*, among other publications. His published plays include: *The Size of the World and Other Plays*, (Billings/Morris, London, 1997), *The Shoreham and Other Plays*, (Whitman Press, 2002) and *ADOPT A SAILOR*, (Bakers Plays, 2004). WILDERNESS OF MIRRORS is the first play in a trilogy he has written about spies and spying. The second play, CLOUDS HILL, was recently presented by The Manhattan Theater Club in a workshop production, directed by David Auburn. The third play, CELADINE, was commissioned by Amy Irving and will premiere at The George Street Playhouse during the 2004-05 season.

Mr Evered is a graduate of Rutgers, Yale University and The Naval Aviation Schools Command in Pensacola, Florida. He is a former officer in the United States Navy, (Res), having served with the Naval Office of Information during the onset of the War on Terror. Currently, he is an Assistant Professor at Emerson College in Boston. He is married to Wendy Rolfe Evered and is the proud father of Margaret and John.

WILDERNESS OF MIRRRORS was first presented at
The Harper Joy Theatre in Walla Walla, Washington
opening on 10 April 2002. The cast and creative
contributors were:

ROBERT ADAIR CONLAN .... Nick Brooks
SUSAN CONLAN .... Hannah Goalstone
CHRISTINA .... Erin Roden
ERIN .... Anna Bullard
JAMES SINGLETON .... Alden Ford
JOEL KIRBY .... Stephen Unckles
WILLIAM GRISWALD .... Sandor Fejervary
SECOND MAN .... Dave Brown
THIRD MAN .... Josh Butchart
COLLEGE STUDENT #1 .... Rebecca Kramer
COLLEGE STUDENT #2 .... Joe Dyer
MAN IN THE GREY SUIT .... Shiv Karin Singh
OTHER MAN .... Ian Danforth

Director .... Morgan Murphy
Scenic design .... Tom Hines
Costume design .... Robin Waytineck
Lighting .... Alan McEwen
Sound .... Kevin Rittner

WILDERNESS OF MIRRORS was given its world premiere professional production at The George Street Playhouse (Managing Director, Mitchell Krieger; Producing Director, George Ryan) in New Brunswick, New Jersey, opening 12 September 2003. The cast and creative contributors were:

ROBERT ADAIR CONLAN ....Michael Countryman
SUSAN CONLAN .... Leslie Lyles
CHRISTINA .... Welker White
ERIN .... Monica West
JAMES SINGLETON .... Alex Draper
JOEL KIRBY *(and others)* .... Yuval Boim
WILLIAM GRISWALD *(and others)* .... Martin Friedrichs

Director .... David Saint
Scenic design .... James Youmans
Costume design .... David Murin
Lighting .... David Lander
Sound .... Christopher J Bailey

CHARACTERS & SETTING

ROBERT ADAIR CONLAN, *a professor at Yale*
SUSAN CONLAN, ROBERT's *wife*
CHRISTINA, SUSAN's *niece*
ERIN, *a student*
JAMES SINGLETON, *a student*
JOEL KIRBY, *a student*
WILLIAM GRISWALD, *a student*
SECOND MAN
THIRD MAN
COLLEGE STUDENT #1
COLLEGE STUDENT #2
MAN IN THE GREY SUIT/CAMPBELL
OTHER MAN

*The play takes place in various times between the years 1942
and 1968. The settings are New York City, New Haven,
Connecticut, Berlin, Germany, Washington D C, Bethesda,
Maryland, and at a safehouse outside Arlington, Virginia,
respectively.*

NOTES ON PRODUCTION

The set should consist solely of a sparse rendering of
the library of the Yale Club in New York City. Parquet
floor, finely appointed shelves lined with books around
the perimeter, etc. Tables and chairs that exist in the
Yale Club in 1968 should be employed to facilitate the
scenes occurring in the past. Like a dream, the past
"materializes" in front of us.

Everything should be done to facilitate the smoothness
of the transitions. The play is meant to flow seamlessly,
in and out of time. In that way, lighting is very
important. Also, the director should feel free to explore
the ways in which some "times" might flow into each
other, even overlap with one another.

ROBERT is only in his late sixties in 1968, so his cane
does not denote a huge disability. Its meant to help the
audience visually understand the differences between
scenes in the past, when he has no cane, and the time
back at the Yale Club, when if he uses it at all he does
so with great ease.

If appropriate, it would be perfectly fine to double cast
some of the smaller roles.

As for props; try to employ as few as possible. There's
no need for real food on the tables or real fishing poles.
Many of the props needed for the scenes in the past
might very well be found in the Yale Club set, on the
shelves, etc.

As for the aging of the characters: For JAMES, SUSAN, CHRISTINA, etc, the use of makeup would be appropriate. While ROBERT doesn't seem to age at all.

"There had to be one man who said, 'yes'. Someone had to agree to captain the ship. She had sprung a hundred leaks; she was loaded to the waterline with crime, ignorance, poverty. The wheel was swinging with the wind. The crew refused to work and were looting the cargo. The officers were building a raft, ready to slip over-board and desert the ship. The mast was splitting, the wind was howling, the sails were beginning to rip. Every man jack on board was about to drown—and only because the only thing they thought of was their own skins and their cheap little day-to-day traffic. Was that a time, do you think, for playing with words like 'yes' or 'no'? Was that a time for a man to be weighing the pros and cons, wondering if he wasn't going to pay too dearly later on; if he wasn't going to lose his life, or his family or his touch with other men? You grab the wheel, you right the ship in the face of a mountain of water. You shout an order, and if one man refuses to obey, you shoot straight into the mob. Into the mob, I say! The beast as nameless as the wave that crashes down upon your deck; as nameless as the whipping wind. The thing that drops when you shoot may be someone who poured you a drink the night before; but it has no name. And you, braced at the wheel, you have no name either. Nothing has a name. Except the ship, and the storm. Now do you understand?"

Creon

Dedicated to the men and women I had the honor of serving with in The United States Navy Office of Information, 2000-2003.

ACT ONE

*(In the darkness, we hear the Yale Whiffenpoofs singing
The Whiffenpoof Song:)*

...we will serenade our Louis while life and voice shall
   last,
Then we'll pass and be forgotten like the rest.
We're poor little lambs who have lost our way:
Baa! Baa! Baa!

*(And as the song continues, the lights fade up, revealing the
library of the Yale Club in New York City, 1968. In a faint
pool of light, semi-obscured, we see the outline of* ROBERT,
*seated. There is a subtle indication he may be an older man,
as he has a hand wrapped around a silver tipped cane and
seems a little hunched.)*

"We're little black sheep who have gone astray:
Baa! Baa! Baa!
Gentlemen songsters off on a spree,
Doomed from here to eternity,
Lord have Mercy on such as we:
Baa! Baa! Baa!"

(The music fades as ERIN, *around twenty, dressed in
"hippie" like clothes, casually walks into the library.
She has a piece of paper and a pencil in her hand and appears
to be searching for a book. As soon as she enters,* ROBERT
*recedes into his chair, as though he doesn't want to be
disturbed.* ERIN *looks over at him, then continues looking
for a book. After a moment, she casually turns to him.)*

ERIN: There's a uh, concert downstairs. The "Whiffs" are here.

(ROBERT *remains perfectly still, no response.* ERIN *continues to look for a book. After a pause, she turns toward him again.*)

ERIN: You'd think the library at the Yale Club would have a better filing system. It's a wonder anyone could find a book at all.

ROBERT: Though of course, they'd have to be looking for one.

ERIN: Sorry?

ROBERT: I said...in order to find a book, someone would have to be looking for one.

ERIN: I am looking for one.

ROBERT: Hmm.

(ROBERT *turns away.* ERIN *starts to leave, then turns back to him.*)

ERIN: I am curious what makes you think...

ROBERT: ...my dear girl, pretense is something only the young have time to endure.

ERIN: Alright. You're right, I'm sorry. It's just that I didn't want to just "announce" myself.

ROBERT: Oh, but you already have. There's no writing on it.

ERIN: On what?

ROBERT: On the piece of paper in your hand— which suggests to me that it's nothing more than an affectation. As is that pencil in your other hand. The one with no point on it. When people walk into library stacks looking for a book—with a piece of paper in their hand, there is almost always something written on it. Something along the lines of say...the Dewey Decimal

System. If there isn't, why would they bother having the piece of paper in their hand in the first place? And so, you did announce yourself. As a person walking into the stacks of a library for some reason... other...than to find a book.

ERIN: I guess I should have been a little more prepared. Considering who I was hoping to meet.

ROBERT: And who would that be exactly?

ERIN: Well, you.

ROBERT: And who would I be exactly?

ERIN: Professor Conlan.

ROBERT: Down the hall, first door on your left.

ERIN: What?

ROBERT: For whom you're looking. Down the hall, first door on your left.

ERIN: Oh, well...I'm sorry to have bothered you.

(ERIN *walks off.* ROBERT *stays perfectly still. After a moment,* ERIN *comes in again, standing in front of him.*)

ERIN: There is no door on the left. And there is no hall.

(ROBERT *starts to grin, then laugh.*)

ERIN: Why are you playing with me like this?

ROBERT: Why are you playing with *me* like this?

ERIN: I just wanted to ask you a few questions.

ROBERT: And I just wanted to avoid being asked them.

ERIN: I'm a student, okay? My name is Erin, and I'm a journalism student over at Barnard. I just wanted to get some information for a story I'm writing about spies and stuff. Now...are you Professor Robert Adair Conlan or not? (*Pause*) Are you the one that recruited all those boys at Yale into becoming spies? Are you the one that...

ROBERT: ...are any of us anyone, really? Am I speaking to you now or is it the projected image I have of myself speaking, and if so, does perception follow the reality or the other way around?

ERIN: Not quite following.

ROBERT: I'm trying to communicate in a manner in which someone from your "generation" might actually understand. You are a "hippie," arent you?

ERIN: I dont really go in much for categorization.

ROBERT: No, of course you wouldnt. This is the "age of Aquarius" after all.

ERIN: Look, I just want to find some things out.

ROBERT: And I just want to avoid being the subject of undergraduate drivel.

ERIN: You're not a very nice man.

ROBERT: *(Dry as bone)* I am "run through."

(She starts to turn away, turns back)

ERIN: Did you take any of them fishing?

(ROBERT slowly looks up, glaring at her. She glares back, then finally starts to leave when suddenly, he calls out to her.)

ROBERT: Sit.

(ERIN stops, surprised. She then reaches into her bag and fumbles for a pen and a notebook. She takes both out. Sets herself to write)

ERIN: How did you know he was the "right sort of man?" I mean, how did you know any of them were?

(Pause)

ROBERT: Like you...they would "announce" themselves.

ERIN: How?

ROBERT: Well, like most meetings, it usually started with a knock.

(On the word "knock" we hear a series of loud, vigorous knocks as lights cross fade revealing SUSAN CONLAN, almost forty, standing in the middle of the living room of an apartment in New Haven, CT, 1942. SUSAN is attractive, with a sharp intelligence in her eyes. Her niece, CHRISTINA, nineteen, stands shyly off to the side as ROBERT turns into the apartment, back in time)

SUSAN: Robert, dont be silly. You can't tell a thing about a person by the way they knock on a door. Now, answer it.

(Another series of loud knocks)

ROBERT: Outgoing, athletic...brash, even.

(Another series of knocks in a goofy rhythm)

ROBERT: Yet not what one would call "overly intellectual."

(SUSAN turns to CHRISTINA.)

SUSAN: Christina, darling, answer the door.

(SUSAN goes in the kitchen as CHRISTINA remains frozen.)

ROBERT: Susan, your niece was too shy to go out and buy me a pack of cigarettes.

CHRISTINA: I got your cigarettes.

(Two more knocks)

ROBERT: From a vending machine.

(Several loud knocks in a row)

ROBERT: Alright, alright!

(ROBERT opens the door. Standing there is JOEL KIRBY in a Yale Letterman's sweater. He's an athletically built young man of about twenty. He eagerly, [Somewhat too eagerly]

shakes ROBERT's *hand, holding flowers in the other.*
We notice he has a slightly deliberate walk.)

JOEL: Professor Conlan. Gee whiz its swell to meet you.

(Finally releases ROBERT's *hand)*

ROBERT: Well...thank you. And you are...?

JOEL: Oh, Kirby, sir. Joel Kirby. I only just got your invitation this morning or I would have had more time to find something more... appropriate to wear.

ROBERT: Yes, well, they were only sent out this morning. Did you follow my instruction?

JOEL: Which was that, sir?

ROBERT: The one about not mentioning the invitation to anyone.

JOEL: Oh, yes, sir. Although I did let it slip just a pinch to my roomie. He caught me off guard as I was stepping out of the shower.

ROBERT: How exactly?

JOEL: Well, he asked me what my "plans were" this evening and...well, it just slipped out.

ROBERT: I see. Well, I dont know many people who could withstand a grilling like that.

JOEL: I'm a little slow in the ol brains department sometimes, sir.

ROBERT: Yes, as your knock previously indicated.

JOEL: My "knock," sir?

*(*SUSAN *re-enters.)*

ROBERT: Oh, my wife...Susan.

JOEL: A pleasure, Mrs Conlan. *(He hands her the flowers.)* These are flowers.

SUSAN: So they are, yes. And this is my niece, Christina.

JOEL: A pleasure, miss.

(CHRISTINA *faintly smiles at him. We hear three mild knocks at the door.*)

ROBERT: Ah, now that's a knock. Circumspect...tactful...

SUSAN: Just answer it, Robert.

(ROBERT *pauses, waits for another knock. None comes*)

ROBERT: And patient...

SUSAN: Robert!

(ROBERT *walks over, opens the door. Standing there is* WILLIAM GRISWALD, *twenty, hawk-like and austere.*)

ROBERT: Mr..?

WILLIAM: Griswald, sir. A pleasure to meet you.

ROBERT: Yes, welcome. Allow me: my wife, Susan, niece Christina and Mr Kirby.

WILLIAM: Nice meeting you all.

SUSAN: How would you boys like a hot chocolate to warm up?

WILLIAM:	JOEL:
Yes, Maam.	Very much, thanks.

(SUSAN *goes into the kitchen as* ROBERT *inspects his watch.*)

ROBERT: It seems a third of you is late.

WILLIAM: Who is that, sir?

ROBERT: "Singleton?"

JOEL: Never heard of him.

WILLIAM: Nor I. Might I ask, sir?

ROBERT: You might.

WILLIAM: Well, it's not that I'm not flattered to be asked here, certainly. Your reputation, particularly your writings on Hawthorne are renowned, but....

ROBERT: ...what are you doing here, is that it?

WILLIAM: Well, yes, sir. I've never had the pleasure of taking one of your classes.

JOEL: Nor have I. Have I, sir?

ROBERT: Something tells me I would have remembered that, Mr Kirby. The reason is quite simple. There's a little library project I'm working on. It involves the acquisition of...books...and I'm looking for a little help with it. Two of you were chosen out of many considered.

(SUSAN *enters with hot chocolate.*)

JOEL: And the third, sir?

ROBERT: Oh, yes. One of you was asked to be considered as a kind of...favor.

WILLIAM: Why was that?

ROBERT: Because one of you has a father who is extremely rich. And a Senator. (*Looking directly at* JOEL) I'll leave it up to the three of you throughout the course of the evening to figure out who that is.

SUSAN: Robert...

(JOEL *turns red, moves off to the side.* ROBERT *seems to suddenly have a feeling. He looks toward the door, slowly walking toward it.*)

SUSAN: What is it?

(ROBERT *suddenly opens the door. Standing there is* JAMES, *twenty, handsome, but with a mournful mysteriousness about him. He extends his hand to* ROBERT)

JAMES: Singleton, sir. James T.

(The lights cross fade as ROBERT *turns forward in time to the Yale Club.* ERIN *is across from him)*

ERIN: Why didn't he knock?

ROBERT: He told me years later he was just about to.

ERIN: And you believed him?

ROBERT *Of course not.*

(Lights cross fade up on the students, SUSAN *and* CHRISTINA, *all having just eaten, with cups in their hands.* JOEL *turns to* SUSAN.

JOEL: Top notch prime rib, Mrs Conlan. And cooked just right, too.

WILLIAM: Here, here.

SUSAN: I'm glad you boys liked it. I hope you saved some room for apple cobbler.

JOEL: Yes, ma'am!

SUSAN: And Robert, remember, just coffee for them. They're not of age yet.

ROBERT: Of course, dear.

*(*SUSAN *exits back into the kitchen as all in one fluid movement,* ROBERT *produces a bottle of scotch.)*

ROBERT: A little cure for what ails you, boys?

*(*JOEL *jumps first.)*

JOEL: Yes, sir!

*(*ROBERT *pours some into* JOEL's *cup.* WILLIAM *steps up next.)*

WILLIAM: Dont mind if I do, sir.

*(*ROBERT *pours some for him, then turns to* JAMES.*)*

ROBERT: Mr Singleton?

JAMES: Thank you, no.

ROBERT: Fair enough. *(He puts down the bottle.)* Alright boys, down to business.

JAMES: I'd like to register my discomfort, sir.

ROBERT: Your what?

JAMES: I'm very uncomfortable with your lying like that.

ROBERT: Like what?

JAMES: You gave your wife every indication you wouldn't serve us any alcohol, then as soon as she left the room...

JOEL: ...hey, lighten up, Singleton.

JAMES: *You* lighten up.

WILLIAM: Simmer down, buddy.

JAMES: *(Fierce, To* WILLIAM*)* I'd prefer not to be addressed in a manner that assumes a familiarity that does not exist.

JOEL: You're being rude, Singleton.

WILLIAM: Yes, you are.

*(*CHRISTINA *suddenly stands.)*

CHRISTINA: No, he's right.

(As the lights cross fade to the Yale Club, where ROBERT *turns forward in time)*

ERIN: It was a set up, wasn't it? The drink, pouring it in their cups. It was a way to test how honest they were. And your wife was in on it.

ROBERT: Of course she was.

ERIN: *(Looking toward* CHRISTINA*)* And the girl— was she in on it, too?

ROBERT: No, in fact I never knew she had it in her.

(The lights cross fade to New Haven again, where ROBERT *turns back in time. The boys are all spread about the room as* CHRISTINA *watches from the side.)*

ROBERT: And so, plans for the future. *(Points quickly)* Kirby!

JOEL: I was hoping to join up, sir. I'd like to kill me some of those Nips or Huns. Maybe some "Eye"-talians, too. I would have joined up already, but it seems I have a little foot problem.

ROBERT: What is that?

JOEL: Well, just what it sounds like, sir. I have... little feet. The doctors, call em "disproportionately diminutive" or some such term like that, as compared to the size of the rest of me. And apparently, the army cares about your feet. Something to do with all the marching they do.

ROBERT: Yes, I imagine that's true. Though I must say, looking at them, they dont seem disproportionate at all.

JOEL: Well, that's because I wear regular sized shoes sir, then stuff 'em with corn husks. In point of fact, my actual feet are less than half the size of the shoes you're all looking at right now.

(Everyone pauses a moment, looking at his shoes. Finally)

ROBERT: Right. Griswald?

WILLIAM: Finance, sir. My grandfather has a firm over in Europe. He says what with the detention of the Jews and all, there's bound to be a killing to be made over there.

ROBERT: Well, what remarkable...foresight? Singleton!

(JAMES and CHRISTINA are caught looking at one another.)

ROBERT: Mr Singleton?

JAMES: Yes, sir?

ROBERT: Plans?

JAMES: Fishing, sir.

(*Everyone laughs.*)

WILLIAM: Did you say "fishing?"

JAMES: That's right.

ROBERT: As an occupation?

JAMES: If at all possible, yes.

JOEL: You can't be serious.

JAMES: Can't I? I can't imagine anything I like better. And why not do what you like most of all?

ROBERT: What is it you like about...fishing?

JAMES: The waiting, mostly. All the work you put into it, and then the waiting. I'm partial to fly fishing mostly. I went for the first time down in West Virginia with my father the summer before he died. He's the one who taught me all the differences and variations between the flies you tie, the colors you use, the shape of things. I love tying them on. Thinking what tiny, almost imperceptible little piece of it just might glimmer or gleam a little...what part of it I'm constructing might catch their eye. And I'll walk... up and down the riverbank having a look at all the different kinds of insects there, all the different species of things all along the ground. Just studying them. Because I know if I replicate that sort of creature exactly, tie it onto my hook, the fish in that particular area will be all the more familiar with it. All the more trusting of it. And so the "catch" for me begins hours— sometimes even days before my line ever hits the water. To tell you the truth the fish on the end of my hook is more of just an afterthought, really. It's the waiting, for me. That's the fun of it.

(*Silence, then*)

ROBERT: Griswald...

WILLIAM: Yes, sir?

ROBERT: Kirby...

JOEL: Sir?

(ROBERT *moves to the door, opens it.*)

ROBERT: It was a perfect pleasure.

WILLIAM: What?

ROBERT: Hop, hop, on your way.

JOEL: But...but...we haven't even had our cobbler yet.

ROBERT: My wife will send a dish to your room.
Shake a leg.

WILLIAM: But...?

ROBERT: Off we go.

(WILLIAM *and* JOEL *unceremoniously exit.* ROBERT *closes the door.* SUSAN *steps out of the kitchen, sees only* JAMES *standing there, smiles at him.* CHRISTINA *smiles at him as well as he looks back at them all, curious.*)

ROBERT: Congratulations, Mr Singleton.

(*The lights cross fade to the Yale Club, where* ROBERT *turns forward in time.*)

ERIN: What did *he* know?

ROBERT: Only what he had to.

ERIN: But that's wrong, isn't it? Leaving someone in the dark like that. Especially about their own future?

ROBERT: Exactly how would one define "wrong?"

(*As the lights cross fade back to the apartment in New Haven, where* SUSAN *faces* ROBERT, *turning back in time*)

SUSAN: ...as in the wrong thing to do, Robert.

ROBERT: But sometimes, darling, one has to do wrong to be right.

SUSAN: But this is a human being you're talking about.

ROBERT: And an exceptional one at that.

SUSAN: He wants a father.

ROBERT: What? What are you...? Don't be silly. I have as much chance of being a credible father figure as you have of giving birth. *(Realizing what he said)* Darling, forgive me.

SUSAN: It's alright, Robert.

ROBERT: Look, I'll...keep trying to be something to him other than...

SUSAN: ...a recruiter?

ROBERT: Yes.

(She touches his cheek, strokes it)

SUSAN: That's my good Robert.

(We hear a doorbell.)

ROBERT: What is that?

SUSAN: It's called a "doorbell." I had it installed because I got so tired of your analyzing everyone's knocks.

ROBERT: Well, that wasn't very nice.

SUSAN: Yes. But, as you would say darling: "Exactly how would one define nice?"

(SUSAN smiles, goes into the kitchen. ROBERT opens the door. It's JAMES)

ROBERT: You're late.

JAMES: Sorry, sir.

ROBERT: "Silence."

JAMES: Sir?

ROBERT: "Silence." Explain silence to me.

JAMES: A state of being—bereft of sound.

ROBERT: That's defining it. I want you to explain it.

JAMES: I...

ROBERT: not in a straight line. Don't think like in school.

JAMES: It's....

ROBERT: Yes?

(JAMES *can't speak.*)

ROBERT: Nothing is coming to you because I can hear the machinery of thirteen years of banal systematic educational indoctrination churning away. You're thinking as though you were a human thought factory again—producing replies, answers and retorts. You need to think in terms of prayers and poems— not conclusions.

(JAMES *closes his eyes)*

JAMES: —a room.

ROBERT: Silence?

JAMES: Yes.

ROBERT: With doors closed or open?

JAMES: Open.

ROBERT: Is it a safe room nonetheless?

JAMES: Comforting.

ROBERT: And the color of the room?

JAMES: All grey—and even.

ROBERT: So silence is an "even grey place." Is that it?

JAMES: Yes, that you could lie down in.

ROBERT: And sleep?

JAMES: Or dream.

ROBERT: So silence is a dream?

JAMES: Yes, an "even grey place".

ROBERT: With doors open...

JAMES: That...

ROBERT: Go on...

JAMES: speaks.

(JAMES *opens his eyes again.*)

ROBERT: "Silence speaks."

JAMES: It's exhilarating talking like this. I don't do this with any other professors.

ROBERT: No, I imagine you dont. Have you studied the Latin?

JAMES: *Certe, studui sententiis Latinis.*

ROBERT: And the Chinese?

JAMES: *Hen rongyi.*

ROBERT: Lovely, now...

(SUSAN *enters, sees* JAMES.)

SUSAN: Hello, James.

JAMES: Hello, Mrs Conlan.

SUSAN: Just getting my sewing.

JAMES: *(To* ROBERT*)* Could we go fishing?

ROBERT: Could we what?

JAMES: Go fishing.

ROBERT: Well...

(SUSAN *conspicuously clears her throat as she retrieves her sewing.*)

ROBERT: Uhm...alright. Why not? Fishing is known for its... something. Now, about those Latin roots...

JAMES: When?

ROBERT: What about fall? That's fishing season, isn't it?

JAMES *It's fall now.*

ROBERT: Is it?

JAMES: What about this weekend?

ROBERT: I can't this weekend.

JAMES: Why? If you don't mind my asking.

ROBERT: Because we have a uh... *(Turns to* SUSAN, *clearly making this up)* a barbecue to go to, don't we dear? The uh...Swensons...?

SUSAN: Oh, no, Robert. That's been canceled, don't you remember? Jenny has a little—tickle in her throat.

ROBERT: *(Glaring at her)* A "tickle." No, I did not know that.

SUSAN: Oh, yes. So that frees you up to go fishing. Why don't you come by early Saturday morning, James? I'll be sure Robert is bundled up all cozy.

JAMES: That's great!

ROBERT: Yes, "great." Thank you sooooo much for your help, darling.

SUSAN: Any time, Cuddly Muffin. *(She smiles a loaded smile toward* ROBERT *and retreats back into the kitchen.)*

ROBERT: Fine, now, when conjugating the Latin...

*(*CHRISTINA *walks in.)*

CHRISTINA: ...Eridanus is out!

ROBERT: What?

CHRISTINA: The constellation.

JAMES: Is that the "Winding River?"

CHRISTINA: You know it?

JAMES: Just from books. Is it rare that it's out?

ROBERT: Excuse me—if you two don't mind—

(SUSAN *enters.*)

SUSAN: Christina!

CHRISTINA: Eridanus is out.

SUSAN: Is it really?

ROBERT: Oh for cripes...

JAMES: ...I don't think I've ever seen it.

CHRISTINA: I was just going up to East Rock.

JAMES: *(To* CHRISTINA*)* Would you mind if I tagged along?

ROBERT: *I* would!

SUSAN: Oh, Robert, let him go.

ROBERT: His verbs are flabby!

SUSAN: His verbs will still be there when Eridanus has gone.

CHRISTINA: We should go before it gets cloudy.

JAMES: Sir, I'd very much like to...

ROBERT: ...go, go! Just review your verbs.

JAMES: I will, sir, I promise.

(JAMES *follows* CHRISTINA *out.*)

JAMES: Good night!(ROBERT *stands defeated.*
SUSAN *smiles warmly toward him.*)

SUSAN: You used to take me up there, you know, to "look at the stars."

ROBERT: Did I?

SUSAN: Hard to believe, I know.

ROBERT: Your little niece has designs on him.

SUSAN: Oh, I think it's the other way around.

ROBERT: Regardless, he can't be distracted.

SUSAN: Robert, for someone so young, you've become such an old fuddy duddy. *(She moves toward him, playing with his tie, starting to stroke his face.)*

ROBERT: I better get some work done.

SUSAN: Of course you better. *(She turns, disappointed.)*

ROBERT: I wouldn't wait up if I were...

SUSAN: ...I wont.

(He collects his papers, turns to her.)

ROBERT: Goodnight, then.

(She faces away. No response. He exits. SUSAN turns toward the closed door.)

SUSAN: Goodnight, then.

(As the lights fade slowly on SUSAN, coming up on CHRISTINA, who is leading JAMES up to the summit of East Rock Park. Above them is the suggestion of a myriad of stars and magical constellations as light spills down upon their young faces. CHRISTINA points skyward.)

CHRISTINA: There, see!

JAMES: Where?

CHRISTINA: It starts there, just to the right of Orion's ankle. See it?

JAMES: I think so.

CHRISTINA: Then it winds along Cetus, there.

JAMES: Wow.

CHRISTINA: Amazing, isn't it?

JAMES: Yes it is. And it is like a river.

CHRISTINA: Homer called it an "ocean stream." The story goes that...do you want to hear it?

JAMES: Very much.

CHRISTINA: Well, Phaethon, who was the son of Helios...

JAMES: ...the Sun God, right?

CHRISTINA: Right. Well, Phaethon kept pestering his father to let him drive the celestial chariot.

JAMES: "Dad, can I borrow the car?"

CHRISTINA: Exactly. Well, Helios didn't trust him enough to hand over the keys. He just didn't think Phaethon was grown up enough.

JAMES: "But dad, I'm sixteen!"

(CHRISTINA *laughs.*)

CHRISTINA: So Phaethon kept pleading and pleading... wearing his father down until finally, his father relented, passing the keys to the chariot over to his son. And it was a beautiful chariot, laden with gold and jewels and all sorts of amazing trinkets and pulled by two gorgeous white horses. *(She points upwards.)* I imagine the horses to be those two, there, just to the left of the Dipper.

(JAMES *however, doesn't take his eyes off her. She feels this and continues on.)*

CHRISTINA: And so off he went, streaking across the skies in his father's chariot. But soon it became evident that he was indeed—way in over his head. He couldn't control the horses at all and shot straight up to the sky... all the way up there...and then plummeted...all the way down, in a harrowing descent...to there. So close to the earth that he set all the fields on fire.

JAMES: Yipes.

CHRISTINA: The problem being that Zeus got wind of this little joy ride.

JAMES: The Big Man himself?

CHRISTINA: Oh, yes.

JAMES: So what did he do, ground him?

CHRISTINA: No, he sent a thunderbolt straight through his heart, killing him instantly.

JAMES: That'll teach 'im.

CHRISTINA: *(Pointing skyward)* And there he fell, straight into the river Eridanus.

JAMES: Gee whiz.

CHRISTINA: And what, Mr Singleton, would you say the moral of that story is?

JAMES: Don't fuck with Zeus?

(She laughs)

CHRISTINA: No. I think the moral is: if you're going to die...and we all will. Die brilliantly. In a beautiful golden chariot pulled by white horses.

JAMES: You're not really the "quiet girl," are you?

CHRISTINA: What do you mean?

JAMES: Well, I've been watching you. And there's a whole symphony of thought going on inside you, only quietly, to yourself. I could see it behind your eyes as you sit there in the corner day after day, watching us.

CHRISTINA: Maybe.

JAMES: The professor can be a bear sometimes. But I think inside he's truly a good man.

CHRISTINA: Oh, he's a challenge, to be sure...and I sometimes worry for my aunt. But there's something else in that house. Maybe its the walls, I don't know, but I feel sometimes like they're all closing in on me. And so I come up here.

JAMES: Where there's no ceiling at all.

CHRISTINA: Only the most ancient one.

(JAMES *walks a little toward her. Takes off his jacket, placing it over her shoulders*)

CHRISTINA: Thank you.

(*His hand lingers on her shoulder. She looks back at him. He moves away.*)

JAMES: Well, we better get back before Zeus notices were gone.

CHRISTINA: Yes, he's not someone we want to make mad.

(JAMES *starts down the hill, then stops. He turns and notices* CHRISTINA, *who remains staring up toward the stars. Almost as though she were having a premonition.* JAMES *calls out to her.*)

JAMES: Christina?

(*The lights fade on* CHRISTINA's *face and come up on* ROBERT *in the Yale Club.* ERIN *is across from him.*)

ROBERT: It's always been my experience that people who know about spying don't write about it.

ERIN: What is it with you Yalies? This sense of entitlement. The point of this country is that there's not supposed to be a royalty.

ROBERT: Yale, my dear girl, was here well before this country was.

ERIN: And I suppose you think it'll still be here long after its gone.

ROBERT: Countries are random lines and colors drawn on a map—while Yale on the other hand...

(He smiles devilishly as the lights cross fade and ROBERT *turns back in time, where he is suddenly fishing next to* JAMES. *They are standing on the bank of Eatons Brook, where* JAMES *is meticulously constructing a fly.)*

JAMES: The idea, sir, is to keep your line moving, so the fish will think it's a fly.

ROBERT: I'm well aware of the "idea," James. When, exactly, were you planning on putting *your* line in?

JAMES: It's not a competitive sport, sir. I don't see the point in rushing.

ROBERT: Are you sure there are fish in this river?

JAMES: Yes, sir.

(A tug on ROBERT'*s line)*

ROBERT: Oh my...

JAMES: Sir?

ROBERT: For goodness sakes—I think I may have myself a—a "whopper?" Is that the correct term?

*(*JAMES *helps him with his pole.)*

JAMES: Here, pull it up—

ROBERT: Oh, she's a "biggie"—is that how they say it?

*(*JAMES *pulls on* ROBERT'*s line.)*

JAMES: Oh, sorry sir—it's just the current.

ROBERT: What?

JAMES: It's not a fish. The current was pulling your line.

ROBERT: Oh, well. Well, that's very disappointing. So, disappointment is part of the fishing lexicon. Is that right?

JAMES: Often a large part of it, yes sir.

(JAMES *goes back to his pole.* ROBERT *settles back into his stance.)*

ROBERT: You know, James—

JAMES: Sir?

ROBERT: It appears as though our trip will be coming up...and rather soon.

JAMES: Really?

ROBERT: Yes. And I feel an obligation to tell you a little more about the nature of it.

JAMES: Am I going to be a spy?

(ROBERT *is taken aback)*

JAMES: I've naturally had my suspicions.

ROBERT: Of course you have.

JAMES: When would we leave?

ROBERT: Anytime.

JAMES: Anytime from...

ROBERT: ...now. Anytime from now.

JAMES: And I mustn't tell anyone?

ROBERT: No, you must not. We've been working together for quite some time now. Soon well be able to put all of that work to good use.

JAMES: So you're not really my friend.

ROBERT: What?

JAMES: It was only that I met certain criteria, that I could be helpful. Even fishing. We're only here because....

ROBERT: ...that's not entirely true, James. I have only the highest regard for you.

JAMES: But you're not my friend.

ROBERT: I don't know what I am. I...we've spent time together...sometimes, one has to see the larger picture.

JAMES: But why, when the smaller picture would do just fine?

ROBERT: You have a great...facility.

JAMES: I feel different from other people.

ROBERT: You are different.

JAMES: But to what end?

ROBERT: You see more shades and colors. More of the places in the mind—in-between the places we think we know. Maybe you and I are alike that way.

JAMES: What would I do?

ROBERT: You'll find out soon enough. But do you understand what I'm asking of you?

JAMES: I think so.

ROBERT: Yes, but will you accept the responsibility? It's an oath. You'll be part of a club, only it will never meet. Do you accept?

(JAMES *looks away, then back at* ROBERT.)

JAMES: I'm scared.

ROBERT: What?

(JAMES *suddenly embraces* ROBERT. ROBERT *stands frozen, not knowing at all how to react.*)

ROBERT: I'm afraid I'm not very—

(ROBERT *slowly allows himself to genuinely embrace* JAMES *back. He then removes his handkerchief and passes it to* JAMES.)

JAMES: Thank you.

(JAMES *wipes his eyes, then blows his nose—loudly into the handkerchief. Suddenly he seems like a little boy as he innocently passes the handkerchief back to* ROBERT.)

JAMES: I accept.

(ROBERT *smiles, relieved. Places his hand on* JAMES *shoulder*)

ROBERT: There's a good boy, James. Now, one little hint about your future travel itinerary: study up on your German.

JAMES: Yes, sir.

(ROBERT *looks back into the river.*)

ROBERT: And are you sure James—that there are fish in this river?

JAMES: Yes, sir.

(JAMES *manages a smile as the lights fade to black and come up on* ERIN *at the Yale Club.*)

ERIN: We're you worried he wouldn't go?

ROBERT: He had little or no interest in it.

ERIN: Which of course made him all the more attractive as a potential agent.

ROBERT: Those who approached us were automatically considered the least desirable. In that way it's like dating.

ERIN: Or a kind of game.

ROBERT: Always a game.

ERIN: Only this boy you cared about.

(ROBERT *remains silent as the lights fade on the Yale Club and come up on* CHRISTINA, *who is standing near a bookshelf in the New Haven apartment. She is perfectly still, reading a piece of paper in her hand. Suddenly,* SUSAN *walks in.*)

SUSAN *Good morning!*

(CHRISTINA *is startled, quickly making an effort to conceal the paper.*)

SUSAN: Oh, I'm sorry. I didn't mean to scare you.

CHRISTINA: Oh no, it's fine.

SUSAN: What is that?

CHRISTINA: What?

SUSAN: Behind your back.

CHRISTINA: Oh, I was just...I was cleaning and...

SUSAN: ...Christina, relax. This is just me asking.

CHRISTINA: I was reaching for the uhm...

SUSAN: ...give it to me.

(CHRISTINA *slowly hands her the piece of paper.* SUSAN *looks at it.*)

CHRISTINA: There really isn't a "library project", is there?

SUSAN: Where did you find this?

(CHRISTINA *points toward a space on the shelf.*)

CHRISTINA: There.

(SUSAN *walks over, replaces the piece of paper exactly where* CHRISTINA *points on the shelf.* CHRISTINA *turns to her.*)

CHRISTINA: James could be killed, couldn't he?

SUSAN: Have you looked at anything else?

CHRISTINA: No.

(SUSAN *slaps her across the face.*)

SUSAN: Don't you *ever* violate our trust again.

(CHRISTINA *remains frozen, in shock. She starts to cry.*)

CHRISTINA: I'm so sorry.

SUSAN: We took you in. We opened our home to you—

CHRISTINA: Aunt Susan I'm....

SUSAN: ...you are *not* to mention what you saw to anyone. Do you understand me?

CHRISTINA: Yes.

SUSAN: Especially James. *(Screaming) Do you understand me!?*

CHRISTINA: Yes!

SUSAN: Alright. Then take a deep breath, Christina. *(Pause)* This never happened.

(SUSAN exits. The lights fade slowly on CHRISTINA as she stands there, in shock, as they fade up on the living room later that day. Drinks before dinner as JAMES stands across from ROBERT.)

ROBERT: For the life of me I don't see why people find it so jocular.

JAMES: Well, sir...it's...it's just funny.

ROBERT: But *why* is it funny?

(SUSAN enters, joining in)

SUSAN: It's the two words together that make it so funny, dear.

ROBERT: "Whale...penis."

(JAMES tries to suppress his laughter.)

SUSAN: See? If it were just the word "whale" or even just the word "penis," it wouldn't be funny at all.

ROBERT: I don't see it.

JAMES: I think the word "penis" is funny all by itself.

ROBERT: But "whale penis?"

JAMES: It's just not two words you hear together very much.

SUSAN: And it isn't something most people collect.

ROBERT: I do not collect whale penises. I collect the petrified cartilage of sperm whales.

SUSAN: Whatever you say, dear.

ROBERT: Craftsman have been fashioning pipes, ashtrays, napkin holders and the like out of it for hundreds...maybe even thousands of years.

SUSAN: Whatever you say, dear.

(ROBERT *suddenly produces a bone colored lighter from his jacket.*)

ROBERT: Even lighters.

JAMES: Gosh, sir, is that whale penis?

ROBERT: No! It just so happens that it emanates from the portion of the whale that most marine biologists agree is located in the generalized area of....

SUSAN: ...the whale's dick.

(SUSAN *and* JAMES *can't hold in their laughter.*)

ROBERT: *What* is so funny?

JAMES: Does a flame come out of it, sir?

ROBERT: What?

JAMES: The whale's penis?

ROBERT: Of course a flame comes...it's not a penis!

(ROBERT *proudly clicks the lighter on, producing a large flame.* SUSAN *and* JAMES *lose it again as* CHRISTINA *suddenly appears, wearing a beautiful blue dress.*)

CHRISTINA: I'm sorry I'm late.

(ROBERT *and* JAMES *both stand.*)

JAMES: Not at all. You look...beautiful.

CHRISTINA: Thank you.

SUSAN: Have a seat, Christina. Your uncle was just showing us his penis, werent you dear?

CHRISTINA: I'm sorry?

ROBERT: My whale penis. Which it isn't.

CHRISTINA: I...see.

ROBERT: *(To* SUSAN*)* And you...you're drinking too much.

SUSAN: The doctor said it's good for my blood, dear.

*(*CHRISTINA *looks to* JAMES.*)*

CHRISTINA: I need some air.

SUSAN: But we haven't eaten yet.

CHRISTINA: I'm not very hungry, thank you. Come on James, lets go.

*(*JAMES *stands, turns to* SUSAN*)*

JAMES: Thank you, Mrs Conlan.

SUSAN: You're quite welcome, James.

*(*JAMES *and* CHRISTINA *both exit quickly.* SUSAN *turns to* ROBERT.*)*

SUSAN: When are you leaving?

ROBERT: Day after tomorrow.

SUSAN: And you're taking James?

ROBERT: Yes.

SUSAN: And you don't know when you'll be back.

ROBERT: Have I ever?

SUSAN: Or *if* you'll be back.

ROBERT: Everything is in order.

SUSAN: Oh yes, order.

ROBERT: And you're drinking too much.

SUSAN: Yes.

(The lights fade on the table and come up on the familiar summit of East Rock Park. CHRISTINA *playfully leads* JAMES *by the hand.)*

JAMES: *(Looking up)* I don't see our river tonight.

CHRISTINA: You're very brave, James.

JAMES: Why do you say that?

CHRISTINA: I mean to volunteer...you know, for the library project.

JAMES: Oh yes, arent I though? Think of all the dusty shelves I'll face, the spilled ink—.

CHRISTINA: Nevertheless. I'm proud of you.

JAMES: Thank you, Christina.

(She turns away.)

JAMES: When you were a little girl you dreamed of white picket fences and a husband who looks like Gary Cooper or some such hunk.

CHRISTINA: On the contrary.

JAMES: Then you dreamed of a prince charming or a knight in shining armor.

CHRISTINA: You don't know me nearly as well as you think you do.

JAMES: Then who *did* you dream of?

CHRISTINA: There was a boy...

JAMES: ...I knew it!

CHRISTINA: Christopher Bilotti. Ninth grade.

JAMES: And he was handsome.

CHRISTINA: Oh, a dreamboat. Buck teeth, bowed legs...

JAMES: Okay—

CHRISTINA: But he had the most beautiful, kind eyes. And he was so much sweeter to the world than it was to him. And as for white picket fences, I never had any interest in all that. The house I lived in with my parents had a white picket fence. I'm not sure how I feel about marriage at all to tell you the truth. Sometimes it seems like an unnecessary strain to put on a relationship. You could see what it's done for my aunt and uncle.

JAMES: But their problem isn't marriage. It's how they conduct their marriage.

CHRISTINA: If I got married and had children, I would insist that my entire family live in a railroad box car.

JAMES *Really?*

CHRISTINA: Oh yes. That way the world would always be moving past us, and we'd have a million things to talk about and everyday would be an adventure.

JAMES: It certainly would.

CHRISTINA: And we'd have dinner for breakfast and desert for starters. And if we wanted to stay in our pajamas all day long there wouldn't be anyone to tell us we couldn't.

JAMES: Nor should there be.

CHRISTINA: And just like in the conventional world, we would have plenty of fancy teas and cocktail parties—only we'd have them in a huge and elaborate tree house and everyone would have to come entirely in the nude.

JAMES: But what about the world of the practical, Christina? You'd have a wedding, wouldn't you?

CHRISTINA: Of course I would.

JAMES: And a ring?

CHRISTINA: Yes, but it would be made from a Wisteria vine.

JAMES: I think you're brilliant.

CHRISTINA: And I think you love me.

JAMES: I do.

(JAMES *swallows hard, turns away from* CHRISTINA, *takes a ring box out of his jacket, takes a deep breath, then turns back again, getting on one knee. She looks at him, totally surprised.*)

JAMES: It's only made of gold, but I promise at the first opportunity to trade it in for a Wisteria vine.

(CHRISTINA *is speechless. She takes the box in her hand. We notice* ERIN *slowly walking around the perimeter of the light, imagining this.*)

JAMES: Please, Christina, marry me. I love you very, very much. I'm hopelessly, awfully, painfully in love with you. I've loved you since the first time I set eyes on you. Even before the time that you were born. I loved you thousands of years ago up until and through this very second. Please, marry me.

CHRISTINA: But you can't love me.

JAMES: Why?

CHRISTINA: Because it's impossible.

JAMES: Why!?

CHRISTINA: Because it's what I want.

JAMES: Why are you so convinced you can't get what you want?

CHRISTINA: Because I never have.

JAMES: Well, this is the exception.

CHRISTINA: No, this must be some sort of mistake. Or a dream.

JAMES: It is a dream.

CHRISTINA: We really shouldn't talk like this.

JAMES: I don't know how else to talk. Just being around you inspires me to tell the truth. Marry me. I'll make you happy and I'll make you used to being loved. And when good things happen to you I'll make it so you're not so awfully surprised. And we could live in a box car, that's fine. And we'll keep the doors wide open and for the rest of our lives we'll have wind blowing through our hair and we could swing from one vine to another straight into our tree house and I promise never to build a picket fence around you and that we'll never be certain of anything, ever, and every day will be an adventure and well have zero social standing and no money and no fancy cars and...

(She kisses him. It lingers. Finally, she breaks it off.)

CHRISTINA: I can't cook.

JAMES: I don't eat.

CHRISTINA: I have no family to speak of.

JAMES: I don't speak to my family.

CHRISTINA: I like to take the lead.

JAMES: I have two left feet.

CHRISTINA: I have no formal education.

JAMES: I have no practical knowledge.

CHRISTINA: And you're leaving.

JAMES: No, I'm not.

CHRISTINA: What?

JAMES: I'm not going anywhere. I've decided against it. The world of library projects isn't for me.

CHRISTINA: But you have such a large life ahead of you.

JAMES: Meet me here tomorrow night. We'll elope. We'll go to Maine and get a license.

CHRISTINA: I don't know. I don't know if....

JAMES: ...just meet me here tomorrow night. *(Looks to the sky)* Under Orion. Under his big stupid ankle. We better get back. *(He starts down.)*

CHRISTINA: Take me to the field.

JAMES: What?

CHRISTINA: I want to be with you.

JAMES: But Christina...I've...I've never.

CHRISTINA: ...neither have I. Take me.

JAMES: But I wouldn't want to give you the impression that my intentions were anything less than...

CHRISTINA: ...James. You need to stop talking...and take me.

(JAMES slowly walks over to her. He takes her hand and tentatively leads her out into the darkness as the lights slowly fade and then come up on ROBERT at the Yale Club. He is standing, looking out a window. From outside we hear the sounds of protesters chanting; "Stop The War!" "Stop The War!" ERIN is standing across from him.)

ERIN: It's a very different world out there nowadays. Very different from the one you came up in.

ROBERT: In some ways.

ERIN: The agency isn't even allowed to recruit on campus anymore.

ROBERT: Oh, they're kicking all kinds of shit our way now. They always do. It comes in cycles, like anything else. But mark my words: you'll like us again. You'll like us again when you need us again. That's been true since the beginning of time.

(*Lights cross fade to the apartment in New Haven, where* SUSAN *is seated with her sewing on her lap and* CHRISTINA *curled up on the floor in front of her*)

SUSAN: You're so young, Christina. Feelings can be so fleeting.

CHRISTINA: I love him, Aunt Susan.

(SUSAN *holds the ring in her hand, looks at it, hands it back to* CHRISTINA.)

SUSAN: It's a very beautiful ring.

CHRISTINA: Please give me your blessing.

SUSAN: It's not my place.

CHRISTINA: Of course it is. You're the only family I have.

SUSAN: If you go through with it, it will have very considerable implications. Especially for your uncle. Robert has worked very hard.

CHRISTINA: But it's not our fault we fell in love. Don't you remember what that was like?

SUSAN: I'm afraid I do.

(CHRISTINA *rests her head on* SUSAN's *lap.* SUSAN *looks over at the door. Has a "feeling." She puts down her sewing, starts to get out of the chair.*)

CHRISTINA: What's wrong?

(SUSAN *moves toward the door.*)

CHRISTINA: What is it?

(SUSAN *turns to* CHRISTINA, *raising her finger to her lips.* SUSAN *stands just in front of the door now, then suddenly turns to* CHRISTINA, *a forced tone in her voice.)*

SUSAN: Christina, darling—have you eaten yet?

CHRISTINA: What?

(All at once, ROBERT *walks through the front door.)*

SUSAN: Why, Robert. What a surprise.

ROBERT: Isnt it.

CHRISTINA: Hello, Uncle Robert.

*(*ROBERT *ignores* CHRISTINA.*)*

SUSAN: Christina, why don't you go to the store. We'll need some milk for breakfast.

CHRISTINA: Yes, Aunt Susan.

*(*CHRISTINA *starts out, then turns and hugs* SUSAN. SUSAN *almost recoils, but politely reciprocates.)*

CHRISTINA: I'll see you later, then.

(No response. CHRISTINA *exits. There's a long, uncomfortable pause until:)*

ROBERT: And how was your day, dear?

SUSAN: Spare me the formalities.

ROBERT: I trust it was most productive.

SUSAN: Christina isn't trying to ruin anything, Robert.

ROBERT: Warm today, I thought.

SUSAN: Everything you mean is between what you say.

ROBERT: If I have to pull a ruse tonight, you're coming for the ride.

SUSAN: What are you talking about?

ROBERT: You helped get us in this situation—you're going to help get us out.

SUSAN: I will not do anything to hurt Christina or James.

ROBERT: Tonight—you play along.

SUSAN: I will *not* be a party to...

ROBERT: ...You will do what I tell you! *(He walks up to her, threatening, inches from her face.)* ...darling.

(SUSAN, disgusted, pushes him away and exits as the lights at the Yale Club come up. ERIN is facing ROBERT.)

ERIN: Did it bother you—who you were becoming?

ROBERT: It had been so long since I knew who I was— it didn't bother me one little bit.

(We hear a doorbell ring. The lights fade on ERIN as ROBERT turns slightly, toward the door back in the New Haven apartment many years ago.)

ROBERT: It's open.

(The door opens slowly and in walks JAMES. ROBERT looks at his watch.)

ROBERT: You're fourteen hours early, James.

JAMES: I'm not going.

ROBERT: I'm very sorry to hear that.

(ROBERT picks up a chair, loudly placing it in front of JAMES)

ROBERT: Have a seat.

JAMES: Wouldn't you like to know why?

ROBERT: Sit.

(They sit across from each other)

JAMES: I don't want you to think I'm not grateful. I am.

ROBERT: Your father used to take you fishing.

JAMES: Yes.

ROBERT: "Apple" of his eye, were you?

JAMES: I suppose.

ROBERT: I myself hail from Superior, Wisconsin. Ever had the pleasure?

JAMES: Never, no.

ROBERT: Oh, it's a lovely place, Superior. Especially in the summer. The problem being of course that summer in Superior lasts about three and a half days.

JAMES: Yes, sir. *(He looks at his watch)* I don't mean at all to rush you, but....

ROBERT: I envy your having had a relationship with your father, James. At most, my father was someone who grunted at me once or twice a day—then at night, would slip into my room and lash the living daylights out of me with a three quarter inch belt.

JAMES: I'm very sorry.

ROBERT: And you asked me whether I was your friend.

JAMES: Yes—

ROBERT: And you took an oath. You swore that you would serve.

JAMES: I did, yes, but....

ROBERT: and is this how friends, no family—treat one another, James?

JAMES: No, but I couldn't predict that I would meet Christina. I didn't know....

ROBERT: —Oh, wait, Christ. I was supposed to pass on a message from her. Damn it.

JAMES: What message?

ROBERT: I should have told you right off. From Christina. She wanted us to tell you something.

JAMES: Tell me what?

ROBERT: I told her to wait for you—that she should tell you herself. It wasn't right, her leaving a message with me. I better get Susan. I'm not good at this kind of thing.

JAMES: What are you talking about?

ROBERT: She left. "All the happiness in the world," she told me to wish you. "All the happiness," she said.

JAMES: There must be some kind of mistake.

ROBERT: No, I don't think so. She seemed to imply that you two had some sort of "date" and that she wouldn't be able to make it. This is awkward for me, James— she must have changed her mind about something.

JAMES: That's impossible. I don't believe it.

(Lights up on CHRISTINA, *up on East Rock, waiting for* JAMES *under the stars. The ring that* JAMES *gave her is on her finger.)*

ROBERT: Maybe you're right. Maybe she—maybe I've got it all wrong. We better check.*(He calls out.)* Susan!? Susan, please come out here?

*(*SUSAN *walks out of the kitchen. She has a glass in her hand.)*

SUSAN: Yes, Robert?

ROBERT: What was it exactly that Christina asked us to pass on to James? Do you remember?

*(*SUSAN *just stares ahead)*

ROBERT: Susan?

SUSAN: She said....

JAMES: ...what!

SUSAN: "Tell him I'm sorry," she said. And "good luck."

JAMES: No, I don't believe that. We had plans.

SUSAN: Maine is off, James. Christina doesn't want to marry you.

(JAMES *is motionless, stunned.* SUSAN *walks over toward him.*)

SUSAN: I am so sorry, James. I'm so sorry.

ROBERT: I'm afraid she's already left town. Maybe once you get back you could go after her. But wait, you're not going, are you?

JAMES: —I'm going.

SUSAN: Robert—

(ROBERT *glares at* SUSAN.)

ROBERT: Are you sure, James?

JAMES: I'm sure.

ROBERT: If it's what you want.

(JAMES *turns, starts toward the door.*)

SUSAN: James...

JAMES: *(Turning sharply)* ...No, it's done. *(Pause)* I'm in.

(JAMES *walks out the door.* SUSAN *looks toward* ROBERT *as the light begins to fade on* CHRISTINA, *and then on the apartment as we begin to make out the sound of bombs being dropped in the distance and of muffled gun fire. Lights come up on a clearing outside of Berlin, where* JAMES, *with a heavy overcoat on, emerges out of the darkness. Following behind him is a* SECOND MAN, *out of breath. He has spectacles on and speaks fluent German.*)

SECOND MAN: *Du gehst zu schnell.*

JAMES: *Du gehst nicht schnell genug.*

SECOND MAN: We are safe now, yes?

JAMES: You'll be fine.

(The SECOND MAN *looks in the direction of the bombs.
Flashes of fire in the distance)*

SECOND MAN: Look what it is your planes do to my beautiful Berlin.

JAMES: Yeah, I'm all broken up about it. Where's the Ruski?

SECOND MAN: He is soon behind.

*(*JAMES *looks up at the night sky. The* SECOND MAN *notices.)*

SECOND MAN: No stars this night.

(Suddenly a THIRD MAN *emerges out of the darkness.* JAMES *reaches for a gun in his pocket, then recognizes the man.)*

JAMES: *Ti dolzhen byt zdyes polchasa nazad. (*You were supposed to be here half an hour ago.*)*

THIRD MAN: *Ya nyemog pereytyi most.* (I couldn't cross the bridge.*)*

JAMES: *Mi seychas yhodim.* (We're leaving now*)*

THIRD MAN: *(Thick Russian accent)* You are a good man.

SECOND MAN: Where will we meet the plane?

JAMES: You don't need to know that.

THIRD MAN: You save our lives.

JAMES: I suppose.

SECOND MAN: You are not frightened? Why is that?

JAMES: Because, I don't care.

(We hear a large volley of bombing in the distance.
JAMES *looks out toward it.)*

JAMES: We have to go. *(To* THIRD MAN, *in Russian)*
Poshli. (Let's go)

(JAMES *runs into the darkness. The* SECOND MAN *follows. The* THIRD MAN *finally follows as well as the lights fade slowly to black, cross fading up on* ERIN *in the Yale Club.*)

ERIN: A job well done.

ROBERT: Yes.

(*Lights cross fade up on* CHRISTINA *under the stars again.* ERIN *gets up, walks toward her, almost as though she could see her.*)

ERIN: And so she must have waited up there all night.

ROBERT: I suppose.

(ERIN *comes to within inches of* CHRISTINA, *almost touching her hair.*)

ERIN: In a way I feel like I was up there with her. She was pregnant with me then.

(ROBERT *turns to her, caught off guard.*)

ERIN: Was he a father I could be proud of?

ROBERT: I wouldn't know what to tell you.

ERIN: I want to know how he died.

(SUSAN *enters the Yale Club, though only* ROBERT *can see her.*)

SUSAN: She has a right to know, Robert.

ROBERT: (*To* ERIN) Meningitis as I recall.

SUSAN: You can't die with every secret.

ERIN: I know what the record says. Tell me the truth.

(*As the lights slowly fade to black we hear* Harry's Theme *by Clannad.*)

END OF ACT ONE

ACT TWO

(Lights come up on ROBERT *at the Yale Club.* ERIN *is across from him.)*

ROBERT: You walk through a door, only to find another—walk through that one, only to find another—walk through that one, only to find a box—opening that, only to find another box inside it. Then you step back, only to realize you've been in a box the entire time— and that every door you've opened has been placed, purposefully, one in front of the other—in the shape of a circle. Placed there only to keep you busy opening them—while through some other door you never dreamed of—lies a hundred different windows to a thousand different doors. And yet here you are, trying to open just one of them.

ERIN: What happened after the war?

ROBERT: Your father was conspicuous in his absence. I heard that he had spent some time in Algeria. That he had done some rather ugly things—for some rather unsavory people. He was in and out of the game, —nowhere. At one point I received information that had him living in the Sahara. I can only imagine whatever I heard was mostly true. As most conjecture is. And then—twenty years later—the book.

(Lights fade on ERIN, *up on a seated* JAMES, *twenty years older. Though he looks much older than that. He is sitting behind a table with a pile of books on it. A nerdy college student addresses an audience.)*

STUDENT #1: I know I speak for everyone here at Georgetown, Mr Singleton, when I offer my heartiest thanks for coming here this evening and reading from your fascinating new book of poetry, "Constellations." I think all of us liked it a real lot. Mr Singleton has graciously agreed to sign individual copies. So, please, line up on our left.

(STUDENT #1 *grabs* JAMES's *hand, shakes.*)

STUDENT #1: Thank you, Sir.

JAMES:That's quite alright.

(STUDENT #1 *exits as* JAMES *turns to a man standing in front of the table holding a copy of his book.*)

WILLIAM: Liked your book.

JAMES: Thank you.

WILLIAM: Can't exactly say I understood it.

JAMES: I can't exactly say I do either.

(WILLIAM *passes a pen and a copy of the book for* JAMES *to sign.*)

JAMES: Anyone in particular?

WILLIAM: Oh yeah, my wife, "Cindy." She really likes this artsy stuff.

JAMES: Good for Cindy.

WILLIAM: You don't remember me, do you?

(JAMES *looks up*)

JAMES: Sorry.

WILLIAM: I didn't expect you would. We were at Yale together. William Griswald?

JAMES: Were we? What class?

WILLIAM: Actually, not a class. You and I were up for the same job at one point. Rumor has it you got it.

(JAMES *begins to remember.*)

WILLIAM: The professor sends his regards by the way.

JAMES: Does he?

WILLIAM: Yes. It seems I've rather fallen into that line of work myself.

JAMES: Really? Well—I'm well out of it. *(He slides the signed book toward* WILLIAM.*)*

JAMES: I hope "Cindy" likes it. Assuming she exists, that is.

WILLIAM: Listen, James...the professor was hoping you could drop him a line.

JAMES: I like your style: out in the open like this. "Conspicuously inconspicuous" we used to call it. And here I thought you liked my book.

WILLIAM: He was hoping you'd give him a call.

JAMES: Like I said, I'm out. And besides, we've been happily out of touch for some time. I wouldnt know where to reach him.

WILLIAM: Now you would.

JAMES: Sorry?

WILLIAM: *(Nodding)* In the pen.

(JAMES *realizes hes holding the pen* WILLIAM *passed him.*)

WILLIAM: Have a good night, James.

(WILLIAM *walks off.* JAMES *gazes at the pen in his hand as the lights fade to black, coming up at the Yale Club where* ERIN *turns to* ROBERT.*)*

ERIN: I don't even know what he looks like. There are no pictures of him, are there? Not from Yale, not even from his little elementary school in West Virginia. I went down there to find one, but one of you got there first. Someone cut out his little face. It's as though he never existed. I do see him in dreams, though, only he's amorphous. He's more of just an outline of a man. But I do imagine him smiling. And still, even to this day, I sometimes think I see him standing at the foot of my bed. Protecting me. *(Pause)* What made you think he would show up?

ROBERT: He had a score to settle.

(As the lights cross fade, coming up on a non-descript office in Washington, D.C. ROBERT turns into it, back in time, as he opens the office door. JAMES is standing on the other side.)

ROBERT: With most people I recognize their knocks. With you I recognize the silence where the knock should be. Can I get you a drink?

JAMES: I won't be staying long.

ROBERT: No, I didn't expect you would.

(JAMES takes in the office.)

JAMES: "Amalgamated Industries?" How wonderfully non-descript.

ROBERT: Oh, I know. All the rage now, covers like this. I knew a fella who had a cover as an ice cream man. Only problem was, he made so much more money selling ice cream than he did spying, he quit the game altogether and went into ice cream full time.

JAMES: Out of the professor business are we?

ROBERT: Oh, quite some time ago. They suddenly noticed I hadn't published in twenty-three years.

JAMES: I trust your wife is well.

ROBERT: I couldn't exactly tell you. We're not together anymore. Last I heard she was drying out in Bethesda.

JAMES: I'm sorry to hear that. I always thought she was too good for you.

ROBERT: Yes, well, that opinion places you squarely in the majority. Anyhow, I never got a chance to commend you.

JAMES: He was a Nazi.

ROBERT: Sorry?

JAMES: The man I got out of Berlin.

ROBERT: So he was, yes.

JAMES: Yes, and apparently not just your garden variety either...but rather an accomplished mass murderer. I did a little inquiring after the fact. But then you knew that all along, didn't you?

ROBERT: It is a rather peculiar service were in.

JAMES: You're in.

ROBERT: Don't think I'm not fully aware of the myriad of contradictions, James.

JAMES: I was recruited into helping a war criminal escape to South America. A man who epitomized all we were fighting against.

ROBERT: You were...*chosen*...because it was believed you had the capacity to understand that. The "war criminal" provided us with information that led us to scores more like him. You know what they say, James: if it's one's job to clean out the outhouse, one must resign oneself to smelling like shit.

JAMES: And where exactly does it stop? I understand "Amalgamated" has taken up spying here at home. Spying on the very people it was given a mandate to protect.

ROBERT: Well, "No one can surprise like a friend."

JAMES:That's a very slippery slope.

ROBERT: Better we be our own worst enemy than the Soviets. At least we know what we're capable of.

JAMES: Don't you understand how insane that sounds?

ROBERT: I need you to pick up a product.

JAMES: Excuse me?

ROBERT: I need you to come back in.

JAMES: The reason I came here was to tell you to *never* contact me again. *(He starts out.)*

ROBERT: I read your book by the way. I've never been much for modern poetry and all that. But not surprisingly, there was a considerable amount of brilliance in it. Juvenile brilliance, but brilliance none the less.

(JAMES turns back.)

JAMES: How generous of you.

ROBERT: There's someone I need you to meet. He requested to meet with you specifically.

JAMES: I find that hard to believe.

ROBERT: No, it's true. In fact he's quite a fan of yours. You see, along with the Nazi, you saved his life as well.

JAMES: The Russian.

ROBERT:That's right. What he has is extremely valuable, James. And it seems you're the only one he trusts.

JAMES: I wish you all the best of luck. Oh...here's your pen.

(JAMES takes it out of his coat, tosses it on ROBERT's desk. Starts to leave again)

ROBERT: Have you seen Christina?

(JAMES stops for a moment, then continues out. ERIN walks back in time, into the office.)

ERIN: My father was a brlliant writer.

ROBERT: He was, yes.

ERIN: There was no way he would go back in?

ROBERT: He never showed his hand.

ERIN: Not to anyone?

(The lights fade in the office and come up on a section of a park in Washington D C. We see CHRISTINA *walking. She appears much older now, worn down. Suddenly* JAMES *appears, calling after her)*

JAMES: Excuse me, miss?

*(*CHRISTINA *turns around, sees him)*

JAMES: Do you...know who I am?

CHRISTINA: Yes.

JAMES: It's wrong of me, I know.

CHRISTINA: Is this a...chance meeting?

JAMES: No. No, I searched you out.

CHRISTINA: I heard you were dead.

JAMES: I'm afraid not. *(Pause)* You're just as beautiful.

CHRISTINA: What is it you want exactly?

JAMES: I don't know exactly.

CHRISTINA: Did you ever think this might be cruel?

JAMES: Cruel? I have been following you. It's true. I thought I could just watch you walk across this park. Honestly, it's all I intended to do. Just to see you. See that you were alright.

CHRISTINA: Why the sudden concern? Are you dying?

JAMES: No more than usual.

CHRISTINA: Probably just watching would've been better. For me anyway.

JAMES: I'm sorry.

(She starts to walk off, then suddenly turns back)

CHRISTINA: But then watching...watching and waiting was what you did best, wasn't it? What you were made to do.

JAMES: I'd like to think I have a few other talents.

CHRISTINA: To be on the outside of something while giving the whole rest of the world the impression you've been on the inside all along. I suppose that is a talent.

JAMES: Maybe not a very useful one.

CHRISTINA: But with you it was worse. You hurt people.

JAMES: Obviously you're angry with me.

CHRISTINA: If only I could summon that level of feeling. I've run all of it back in my mind, over and over, trying to figure out whether any of it was true. All the things you said to me.

JAMES: All of it was true.

CHRISTINA: Then I would say to myself: we were just children, really. We were so young. In the scheme of things, all it is, is insignificant.

JAMES: There was nothing insignificant about it.

CHRISTINA: Really it was all just shadows. And I'm just a shadow as well. All of us are. I don't blame you, James.

JAMES: Blame me for what?

CHRISTINA: It wouldn't have worked anyway.

JAMES: You don't know that.

CHRISTINA: No, I do. It all worked out in the end. In point of fact I'm not a well person. I've actually become somewhat— (*She suddenly stutters awfully.*) —f...f..f...fr... fragmented. I would have been an embarrassment to you. See?

JAMES:That's not true.

CHRISTINA: N...n...no, it is. I'm not as smart as you. I never was. He knew that. He was right. I only would have held you back.

JAMES: Who are you talking about?

(*She seems not well, distracted, suddenly turning away*)

CHRISTINA: Do you remember Eridanus?

JAMES: Of course I do.

CHRISTINA: Did you know that every second, every hour, every day, a stars light d...d...d...d

JAMES: ...Christina, it's alright...

CHRISTINA: ...diminishes, every second of every day.

JAMES: Why don't we go somewhere?

CHRISTINA: Someday even the sun will go dead black. I have a daughter.

(*JAMES steps back, thrown.*)

JAMES: Do you? Well, that's...that's wonderful. Who's the— lucky man?

CHRISTINA: A...man.

JAMES: Well, how old is she...your daughter?

CHRISTINA: A teenager.

JAMES: Do you have a picture?

(CHRISTINA *doesn't know how to respond.*)

JAMES: It's alright if you don't.

(CHRISTINA *takes a picture out of her purse, hands it to him.* JAMES *looks at it.*)

JAMES: She's.... *(He examines it. For a moment seems perhaps to recognize something in it)* She's very beautiful.

(She takes the picture from him)

JAMES: There are so many things I wanted to say to you.

CHRISTINA: I really should go. *(She starts to leave.)*

JAMES: Christina, please...

(She turns suddenly.)

CHRISTINA: ...for years I would think I saw you. Just flashes, fragments. Someones hair, or the way someone would walk or I'd see you coming out of a cab. You were like a ghost inside of everyone. Popping, popping, popping, from one person then into another— but all of it between places. I would try to imagine what color your hair turned or whether you would ever be able to tie your tie straight, whether you were eating or taking care of yourself or whether you were dead. I wondered what your voice might sound like or how...

(She's trembling, grabbing at his lapel, speaking in whispers, then shouts. JAMES is horrified.)

JAMES: Christina...

CHRISTINA: But then I tr...tr...tr...

JAMES: ...its alright.

CHRISTINA *(Shouting, screeching) I trained my mind!* ...I trained my mind to find a way to distance itself. I imagined that who I was then...with you...was a body my soul used to inhabit, but doesn't anymore. And I would float above myself—looking down, separate from that old part of myself. And that's what I've done for years...floated like that...becoming more and more apart from myself. And from you.

JAMES: You don't need to do that anymore.

CHRISTINA: But now I can't help it. *(She laughs, slightly at first, then building until it's almost uncontrollable. Then it turns to crying. Then she suddenly stops.)* You see I ca... I ca...I can't bring the two parts together anymore.

JAMES: Christina...

(She suddenly puts her hand on his cheek)

CHRISTINA: Shhhh James. It's alright. It's alright. *(She kisses him.)* I wish you all the happiness.

(She turns and walks away, disappearing from view as JAMES watches her go until the lights fade at the same time they come up on ERIN at the Yale Club. She turns to ROBERT)

ERIN: Little by little he was working his way toward who he was. He wanted to identify his own reflection.

ROBERT: And so it seems—does his daughter.

ERIN: I'm trying.

(As the lights cross fade, coming up on a sparse hospital room in Bethesda, Maryland. We see the figure of a woman in a robe sitting in the half light, facing away. JAMES walks into the room. A small bouquet of flowers in his hand. He's tentative at first, then:)

JAMES: Mrs Conlan?

(SUSAN turns around. She's spent, sunken and pale. She squints in the direction of JAMES.)

SUSAN: Who is that?

JAMES: An old friend.

(SUSAN gets up, walks a little closer. Stops in front of him)

SUSAN: Oh my...am I seeing ghosts now?

JAMES: I hope not.

SUSAN: I've wondered for so long....

(He hands her the flowers.)

SUSAN: Oh, they're beautiful. Thank you. *(She holds onto them.)* How did you know I was here?

JAMES: I heard you were...resting.

SUSAN: Oh, "resting."That's a nice one. You have no idea —as you get older, how much you come to appreciate euphemisms. "Maturing" rather than "aging." "Flamboyant" rather than "drunk".

JAMES: Anyway, here I am.

SUSAN: The ever resourceful James.

JAMES: Yes. *(Pause)* So...how are you?

SUSAN: Well, the doctor said that my liver is the size of a rugby ball. Never having seen one I naively inquired as to whether a rugby ball was large...and apparently they are. Other than that I'm peachy. What about you?

JAMES: I'm...fine.

SUSAN: "Fine" as a euphemism for "awful" or "fine" as in fine?

JAMES: I'm...fine.

SUSAN: You look older.

JAMES: I am older.

SUSAN: But older than you should.

JAMES: I don't think I was ever young.

SUSAN: I'm so sorry about so many things.

JAMES: I'm the one who should be sorry. I should have kept in touch.

SUSAN: What would have been the point? I would have been too drunk to notice. *(Pause)* So, "poet." Tell me your life as a poem. I don't want to hear a sob story. Just the essence.

JAMES: As a poem?

SUSAN:That's right. I'll bet you I could encapsulate my last twenty years into a poem, pronto. Want to hear?

JAMES: Okay.

SUSAN: Alright, here goes: "Twenty Years." Poetic ramblings by Susan Conlan. *(She sets herself, then)*:
Glug...glug...glug...
hate...hate...hate...
Woe is me woe is me woe is me.
Glug...glug...glug."
(She turns to JAMES.*)* What do you think?

JAMES: "Astonishingly concise."

SUSAN: And you?

JAMES: Well, mostly I wandered...

SUSAN: ...in a poem!

JAMES: Alright, a poem.*Twenty Years*. A not so epic postmodern postulation by James Singleton:

"Oh fleeting youth...

SUSAN: Oh, yes.

JAMES: "...fear...
tetherless panic and gloom.
Sex against any wall
Poverty.
Glug...glug...glug...

SUSAN: Plagiarist!

JAMES: And—resignation..."

SUSAN: Hmm.

JAMES: What made you give it up?

SUSAN: You mean drinking or the husband?

JAMES: Both.

SUSAN: The husband was easy. The booze on the other hand. *That* was a love affair.

(JAMES *laughs.*)

SUSAN: Actually, in the end...for me...it was a Persian wedding ceremony. Ever been to one?

JAMES: No, come to think of it.

SUSAN: My second cousin was marrying the son of an oil sheik. Oh, the music, the gowns. This particular ceremony however, revolved around the bride dipping her finger into a golden chalice of honey, you know, signifying the "sweet elixir of life" and all that. And the groom...he ever so delicately...sensuously even, took her honey dripping finger and lifted it to his mouth... sucking on it...along with all the sweet hopefulness their long lives had to offer.

JAMES: And that made you quit drinking?

SUSAN: Oh, no. You see it just so happened that this particular bride had on one particularly large...and loose...fake finger nail.

JAMES: Oh...kay.

SUSAN: And so...when the groom started sucking away at the sweet elixir of life, he sucked so hard he dislodged the nail from her finger and ..thoooop...right into his windpipe.

JAMES: You made that up.

SUSAN: If only. And then it began. Almost as if it were in slow motion and amid all this dancing and thunderous applause, I was the only one seeing what was really going on. The strange look on the groom's face, everyone clapping, his hands, clutching his throat, and then *kaplatt*...flat on his face. Dead as a doornail.

JAMES: You...cannot...be serious.

SUSAN: Oh, I'm serious.

JAMES: That is...oh my God, that is...Oh my God...

SUSAN: I don't know, maybe I'm just a "glass half empty" person, but I thought it ruined the entire wedding.

JAMES:That's the worst thing I've heard in my entire life.

SUSAN: Oh, but it gets worse.

JAMES: *How!?*

SUSAN: Apparently, after everyone started noticing the groom was seventeen shades of magenta...screams started echoing out...long, ear-piercing screams from every corner of the ballroom...except one...where apparently, a very distinct "chuckle" could be heard. A chuckle which then apparently graduated into an all out "guffaw"...

JAMES: You were laughing?

SUSAN: Oh, not just laughing. As described to me later, I was "busting a seam."

JAMES: Like nervous giggles at a funeral.

SUSAN: Right, only in this case it was a wedding, and the groom had just choked to death on his wifes fingernail. But other than that, pretty much the same thing.

JAMES: Oh...my...God.

SUSAN: And so here I sit. Giving it the "ol' college try" one more time.

JAMES *(Serious)* I'm proud of you.

SUSAN: Thank you. *(Pause)* So, have you seen Him? And that's a "Him" with a capital "H" by the way.

JAMES: Yes. He found me.

SUSAN: I'm sure you more than held your own...this time. Though you know James, Robert did care about you very much. More than I think he would ever admit.

(JAMES *turns away.*)

JAMES: I know about Christina.

SUSAN: Oh...I can't tell you how relieved I am to hear that. I didn't want to be the one to tell you.

JAMES: How did it happen, do you know? Was it...gradual...or...

SUSAN: I'm not exactly sure. *(Pause)* There is a service tomorrow night, though.

JAMES: What..."service?"

SUSAN: Well, it's just for one night. Family and close friends.

JAMES: Susan...what are you talking about?

(She starts to realize.)

SUSAN: Oh my God...you don't know.

JAMES: "Dont know what?!" What are you talking about!?

SUSAN: Christina is dead. She drowned.

JAMES:That's impossible. I just saw her two days ago.

SUSAN: No, yesterday. I'm so sorry. I just assumed. James, please. I'm so sorry. She loved you very much.

JAMES: She rejected me.

SUSAN: She never rejected you. There are so many lies.

JAMES: What lies?

SUSAN: They're killing whats left of me.

JAMES: Susan, what "lies?"

(SUSAN *stares back at him as the lights fade to black and come up on Erin in the Yale Club. We see the "younger"* CHRISTINA *appear under the stars, looking up at them dreamily.*)

ERIN: She just "walked" into the Potomac River. As calmly as if she were strolling through the park. When a man asked her where she was going, she turned and smiled...

CHRISTINA: ...I'm following the ocean stream.

ERIN: ...she said. And disappeared.

(CHRISTINA *turns, looks toward the daughter she left behind. They stare toward one another as the lights fade on* CHRISTINA *and we hear Three loud knocks on a door. Then three more as the light fades on* ERIN *and* ROBERT *turns back in time to his D C office. We now hear a succession of loud knocks as he walks over to the door. Opens it. Standing in the doorway is* JAMES. *He has no expression on his face.*)

ROBERT: Who would have guessed? What with all the knocking.

(JAMES *says nothing.*)

ROBERT: Come in.

(ROBERT *turns, hovering near his desk.* JAMES *walks inside, then turns and closes the door to the office, conspicuously locking it from the inside.* ROBERT *notices this, obviously uncomfortable.*)

ROBERT: So...does your coming back mean we have a chance of procuring your services once more?

(JAMES *just stares at him.*)

ROBERT: Well, clearly we're not in a very talkative mood.

(JAMES *walks toward* ROBERT. ROBERT *moves away from him. More silence. Finally,* ROBERT *can't take it any more.*)

ROBERT: I take it you've talked with my wife.

(JAMES *continues to stare.*)

ROBERT: I wouldn't trust the ramblings of a recovering alcoholic, James.

(*All in one frighteningly fast move,* JAMES *expertly grabs a fountain pen off the desk and holds it flush against* ROBERT'*s jugular vein.*)

JAMES: I should kill you.

ROBERT: Think, James. Is my life even worth taking?

(JAMES *slowly lowers the pen—slamming it down on the desk.*)

JAMES: *You* drove her to kill herself, not me! I was a boy who wanted a father and *you* took advantage of that.

ROBERT: "Took advantage of it?" How exactly? By taking a backwoods West Virginia scholarship student and giving him opportunities to change the course of history?! Was that "taking advantage" of you?

JAMES: You had no right to change the course of my life.

ROBERT: There are people out there that want to destroy us! And we will find ourselves caught with our pants down. Is that what you want?

JAMES: I want *never* to be like you.

ROBERT: The problem with you, James, is that you'll never reconcile the many ways in which you are! (*Pause*) There are advantages you know, to living i
 the shadows. To always being between two worlds, to never really having a face. So much of the pain never seems to stay with you because you're always moving. And after awhile, after you've accumulated enough names and faces and years behind you, they all just blend into one. And that's the face you see in the

mirror. And though it's not a familiar one—it is yours nonetheless.

JAMES: Christina was above all that. Christina didn't...

ROBERT: ...Christina was a threat.

JAMES: *I loved her!*

(Pause)

ROBERT: Like I said, James...she was a threat. *(Pause)* Come back in.

JAMES: It's too late.

ROBERT: I can brief you myself.

JAMES: No...I mean it's too late. I'm already in.

ROBERT: What are you talking about?

JAMES: My old friend from Russia. I went and found him myself.

ROBERT: You were never a very good bluffer, James.

JAMES:That's why I never bluff.

(ROBERT is clearly very concerned. He slowly turns back to his desk. Lifts up the phone and dials four digits, quickly.)

ROBERT: *(In phone)* Status, please. Yes, I wanted to check on...yes, I do. *(He pulls a piece of paper out of his pocket, reads from it.)* "Quatro"..."Carol".... *(There's a long pause. Then we see his expression change.)* I see. Thank you.

(ROBERT slowly hangs up the phone. JAMES walks over to him, within a couple inches of his face.)

JAMES: I want you to look at me when I tell you this. I'm going to use every skill, every nuance of every talent you ever taught me... and I'm going to destroy you with it.

ROBERT: Give me what he gave you.

JAMES: I'm going to make you...and the Soviets...wish they never started playing in the first place.

(JAMES *starts out.* ROBERT *calls after him.*)

ROBERT: You'll have enemies on two continents. The Soviets will find out you're on your own, and they will come after you. I won't be able to protect you.

JAMES: If what you've been doing to me my whole life has been "protecting me," —I can't tell you what a relief it is to hear you'll stop.

(JAMES *walks through the door as* ROBERT *stands alone.* ERIN *appears in light and turns to him.*)

ERIN: Why didn't you go after him?

(*The light in the office fades as* ROBERT *finds his cane and turns back to her.*)

ROBERT: I had ten men around the building within seven seconds.

ERIN: What happened?

ROBERT: He was never seen. He was always more talented than I gave him credit for.

ERIN: The student had surpassed the teacher.

ROBERT: Long ago.

(*The lights fade on the Yale Club and slowly come up on* JAMES *sitting behind a table. He is seated casually, a wine glass in one hand. Across the room is a* MAN IN A GREY *suit, also holding a glass of wine. The man speaks with a thick Russian accent.*)

MAN IN GREY: In musical terms it's plenty simple, exquisite even. Aria is sarabande, rather like a... how you say, "dance," yes? Of repeats, *da*? Entire variation...consists only of two parts...however, equal length sixteen bars each. How you say? "Symmetrical," no? All throughout. Brilliant.

JAMES: Do you play piano?

MAN IN GREY: Yes, but only in part time. Just for fun, da?

JAMES:That's wonderful. But don't misunderstand me. I do think the *Variations* are brilliant. I'm not arguing their validity, not at all. It's just Bach himself I have a problem with. Just a little too happy go lucky for me. Too connected. Plus I don't trust people who marry their cousins.

MAN IN GREY: You like only sad music, yes?

JAMES: I don't mind if the music is happy. I just think it's a composers obligation to be a sad, grouchy bastard. Bach was too much of a flattering social climber. A court kiss ass.

MAN IN GREY: Not like our Rachmaninov, yes?

JAMES: Now that's a composer! Miserable, depressed—

(The man turns, looking at a small stack of records.)

MAN IN GREY: Aha! You fortunate today. We got both.

(The man puts a record on a portable record player. Starts it. We begin to hear the famous opening aria of J S Bach's Goldberg Variations. *He turns toward* JAMES.)

MAN IN GREY: After this, Rachmaninov.

JAMES: After this. Yes.

(The man suddenly seems a little uncomfortable)

MAN IN GREY: Now...uh...we must as they say: "get back to work."

JAMES: Of course.

(The man reaches for a tiny bell on the table, rings it. In walks ANOTHER MAN *to the table where* JAMES *is sitting. He starts to clear it. As he does this, he roughly pushes the table away from* JAMES *and we notice that in fact,* JAMES's

*other hand is handcuffed to the back of the chair. The man
then brusquely snatches the empty wine glass away from*
JAMES *and exits. Just as he does, the* MAN IN GREY *walks
over to* JAMES, *and as the beautiful aria continues, viciously
pulls* JAMES's *arm back—causing a great amount of pain,
handcuffing that arm to the back of the chair as well. He then
drags* JAMES *and the chair toward the middle of the room and
then turns away, pulling a pair of rubber gloves out of one of
his pockets and slowly beginning to put them on. He looks
over at* JAMES.)

MAN IN GREY: It was very beautiful day today.

JAMES: Was it?

MAN IN GREY: *Da*...very little clouds today.

*(The "Other" man walks in again, this time carrying a tray.
On top of the tray are three surgical "implements." The other
man starts to slowly place each of the items on the table in
front of* JAMES. *The aria continues as the* MAN IN GREY
looks off, distracted.)

MAN IN GREY: Beautiful day.

(As the aria fades gradually and JAMES *stares straight
ahead as the lights fade, coming up on* ERIN *at the Yale Club.
The Third Movement* of Rachmaninov's Suite No 1
(Fantasie), Op 5 *begins to play under.)*

ERIN: If the Russians could get to him, why couldn't
you?

ROBERT: We tried. I can assure you.

ERIN: How long did they have him?

ROBERT: Long enough.

(As the lights go down on ROBERT *and cross fade up in the
safe house again. The Rachmaninov continues as we see*
JAMES *seated in the same chair, a strangely calm expression
on his face. He is staring into the darkness where we see the
outline of what appears to be a young woman standing across*

from him. As the lights slowly come up, we begin to make out the figure of CHRISTINA, *only it's the* CHRISTINA *we met long ago, young and luminous in a brilliant white dress that is the exact same style as the dress she wore the night* JAMES *proposed to her.)*

CHRISTINA: Do you remember the first time you saw me?

JAMES: Of course I do.

CHRISTINA: I was too shy to even look at you.

JAMES: You were sitting in the corner.

CHRISTINA: I was always sitting in the corner.

JAMES: But you're not really here, are you?

CHRISTINA: No, but you must keep your mind trained on me.

JAMES: What are they doing?

CHRISTINA: They're doing things to your body. Only to your body. But if you stay with me—if you keep your eyes and your mind focused, you won't feel it anymore.

JAMES: I'm so tired.

CHRISTINA: I love you very much. *(She walks over to him, caresses his face.)* Stay with me James...

(She disappears as the Suite *continues and the lights fade on* JAMES *and come up on* ERIN *at the Yale Club.)*

ERIN: Did you ever see him again?

ROBERT: Not alive, no. *(He starts putting on his coat and hat.)*

ERIN: Are you telling me the truth?

ROBERT: Of course I am.

*(*ROBERT *slowly turns from the Yale Club and starts walking back in time, into the darkness, moving into the safehouse*

and stopping right in front of JAMES. *The music stops as*
JAMES, *his head hanging between his knees, slowly begins to
look up.* ROBERT *removes his hat.* JAMES *peers through the
shadows as he recognizes* ROBERT. *We see how bad hes been
tortured. Suddenly,* JAMES *starts to laugh, quietly at first,
then gradually building into a loud, mad and grotesque
torrent of laughter mixed with crying.* JAMES *glares toward
the* MAN IN GREY *and the* OTHER MAN *as he continues to
laugh.* ROBERT *stands in front of him, expressionless.* JAMES
finally catches his breath, looking up.)

JAMES: My own country.

ROBERT: Like I said, it's a peculiar service were in. *(He
nods toward the* MAN IN GREY.*)* What did you think of
Campbell's Russian accent?

JAMES: Hey, not bad.

ROBERT: Campbell is from right here in Virginia.
Say "hello" to James, Campbell.

CAMPBELL: *(Now perfect English)* Hello, Mr Singleton.
I wrote a paper about you at the training academy.
Nothing personal, you know.

JAMES: Of course not.

ROBERT: They have what they call "analysts" now. Little
pin heads that never set foot one in the field. They were
sure you were more likely to spill to the Soviets. The
thing about analysts though? They are never right.

JAMES: You gave it a shot.

ROBERT: Yes, we did. *(To* CAMPBELL*)* Could you give us
a moment?

CAMPBELL: Of course.

*(*CAMPBELL *nods to the* OTHER MAN, *and they both walk
out.)*

JAMES: You're going to have to give the nod.

ROBERT: It shouldn't come to that.

JAMES: I'm going to make it come to that.

ROBERT: All I want is the information our Soviet friend gave you, James. But if you don't give it to me, and I let you go...

JAMES: ...I'll go to the real Soviets and blow his cover.

ROBERT: And if the Soviets had gotten to you first?

JAMES: I'd find a way to burn them as well.

ROBERT: And if neither side had caught you: The Soviets or us?

JAMES: I was thinking maybe *The Washington Post.*

ROBERT: And so James is a loose cannon.

JAMES: In every way.

ROBERT: James, what I've done...couldn't you at least try to understand...

JAMES: ...no, I couldnt.

ROBERT: I'm not effusive——I know that. I was an awful husband, that's true. I coerced you into a life you shouldn't have had to live, that's true. I did what I did with you and Christina...I'm sorry, but please...

JAMES: You're wasting your breath.

ROBERT: When I call those men in again I won't be able to talk to you like this. I'll have to be myself again.

JAMES: Which "self" would that be?

ROBERT: It's a dirty rotten business, it is. And if I told you I tried to be a father in my own pathetic way...of course you shouldnt believe me. If I told you how hurt I was that for almost twenty years you disappeared without a word—of course you shouldn't believe me. And if I told you I prayed for your safety. Yes, that's right, *prayed*, you wouldn't believe that as well, would you? And who could blame you? It's my problem after all. It's all the faces I've collected along all the roads I've traveled. I must be telling you this just to get the information I need. I must be begging you, pleading with you, because I want something from you. Is that it? Or could it be...just for the sake of argument, is there even the slightest chance...that I could be trying to save your life?

JAMES: I won't blame you.

ROBERT: James, please...

JAMES: Give them the nod. It's alright. (*He looks at* ROBERT, *sincerely.*) It's alright.

(*Pause as* ROBERT *stares back. Then suddenly screams*)

ROBERT: *Campbell!*

(CAMPBELL *enters.*)

CAMPBELL: Sir?

ROBERT: I'm afraid there's nothing else to say.

CAMPBELL: I'm sorry to hear that, sir.

ROBERT: Close it up.

CAMPBELL: Yes, sir.

(ROBERT *puts his hat back on and moves to leave. He stops, turns back to* JAMES *as though he's about to say something, but doesn't. He looks at* CAMPBELL *and nods, then disappears into the darkness as* CAMPBELL *moves to within inches of* JAMES, *removing a wire from his pocket to strangle him with as the lights bump to black, cross fading up on* ERIN *and* ROBERT *at the Yale Club.* ROBERT *is still in his hat and coat, seated once again. We hear the Whiffenpoofs once more.*)

ERIN: They're singing again.

ROBERT: Yes.

(She turns back to ROBERT.*)*

ERIN: So the Soviets never broke him.

ROBERT: Never.

ERIN: My father was a hero.

ROBERT: A "hero." Yes.

(She turns around, begins to collect her things. Turns back to ROBERT*)*

ERIN: And is that all? Is that the whole story?

ROBERT: The whole story.

(She starts out again, then suddenly turns, steps forward and kisses him on the cheek. ROBERT *looks at her, speechless.)*

ERIN: Thank you.

*(*ERIN *exits.* ROBERT *remains frozen as a single pool of light remains on him. A young* CHRISTINA *in her brilliant white dress appears to retrieve* JAMES—*who is still seated in the chair he was killed in.* CHRISTINA *touches his cheek and* JAMES *looks up, smiling brilliantly as suddenly Eridanus is illuminated above, along with a myriad of other stars as the light on* CHRISTINA *and* JAMES *fade.* ROBERT *remains seated in his chair, perpetually haunted, as we hear the final strains of* The Whiffenpoof Song:*)*

"...doomed from here to eternity,
Lord have mercy on such as we"

(And the lights on ROBERT *fade, until there is only darkness.)*

END OF PLAY